Published by b small publishing ltd.
www.bsmall.co.uk

Text and illustrations copyright © b small publishing ltd. 2022

1 2 3 4 5   ISBN 978-1-913918-22-4

Written, Designed and Illustrated by Kim Hankinson.
Editorial by Jenny Jacoby.

Printed in Malta by Gutenberg Press Ltd.

British Library Cataloguing-in-Publication Data.
A catalogue record for this book is available from the British Library.

We USE SCIENCE

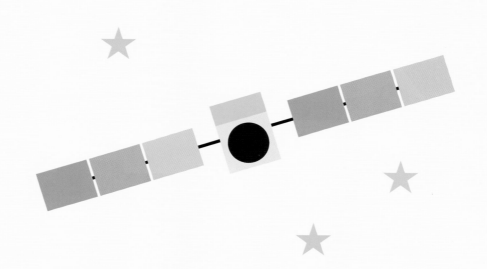

BY KIM HANKINSON

with STEM Editor

JENNY JACOBY

Meet the Everyday Scientists

Firefighter

Briiiiiiiiiiiiing! At the sound of the bell we slide down the pole, put on our gear and head out to an emergency! That might be putting out a fire, helping at a road accident, or rescuing a trapped animal. Some firefighters in hot, dry places battle huge wildfires in fields and forests.

We keep our **fire-resistant** uniforms ready and waiting so that we can pull them on in seconds, because time is very important in an emergency. Sirens on our red fire engines tell the other drivers to let us through. Our trucks are fitted with lots of cool kit, such as the super soaking hoses we attach to hydrants. These spray hundreds of litres of water a minute.

Battling blazes is made safer by new technology but it is still dangerous. When we are close to a fire, we wear masks because the ash in smoke can make it hard to breathe and some materials release **poisonous** gases as they burn.

We always have a plan to fight the fire based on our knowledge of how fires behave, and fires are best fought with teamwork!

We understand the science of fire so we know how to best battle a burning blaze!

You should always go outside when a smoke alarm sounds, even if you don't see fire. Our number one rule is always have a working smoke alarm!

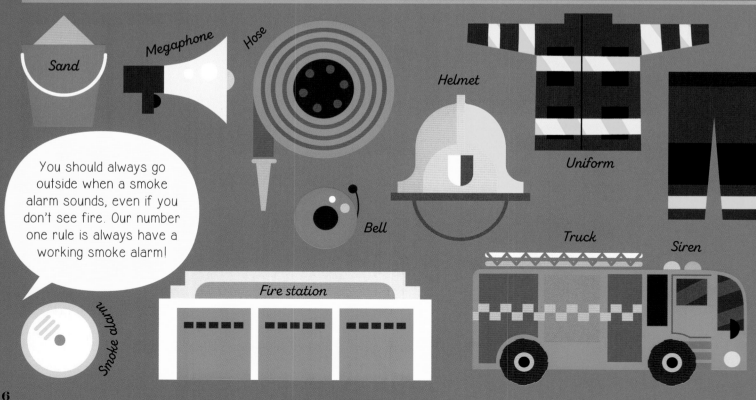

Sand

Megaphone

Hose

Helmet

Uniform

Bell

Truck

Siren

Fire station

Smoke alarm

THE FIREFIGHTER'S FORMULA

THE FIRE TRIANGLE

A fire needs three elements to burn. Without all three a fire will go out, so fire extinguishers work by removing one of these elements.

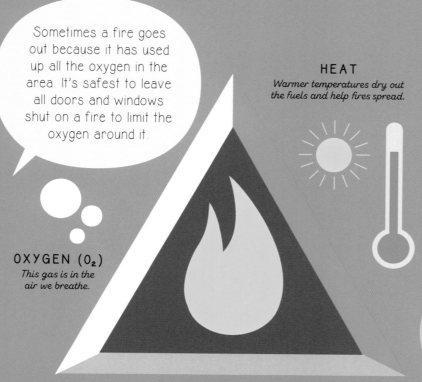

> Sometimes a fire goes out because it has used up all the oxygen in the area. It's safest to leave all doors and windows shut on a fire to limit the oxygen around it.

HEAT
Warmer temperatures dry out the fuels and help fires spread.

OXYGEN (O_2)
This gas is in the air we breathe.

FUEL
This could be lots of things like paper, oils, wood, gases, fabrics, liquids, plastics or rubber.

HOW WE FIGHT A FIRE

Have you noticed lots of different coloured fire extinguishers in public buildings? Although they all work by **smothering** the fire to put it out, they contain different things for different fires. Water is good for putting out fires of burning wood, paper, cloth, plastic or rubber. But water is not good for putting out fires from flammable oil or gas, as it can spread the fire out. Water shouldn't be used on an electrical fire either as water is a **conductor**, which means that electricity shoots through it and can deliver a very bad electric shock.

THE EXTINGUISHERS

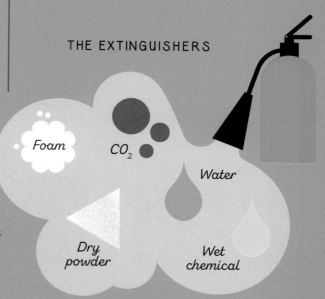

Foam

CO_2

Water

Dry powder

Wet chemical

Walkie-talkie

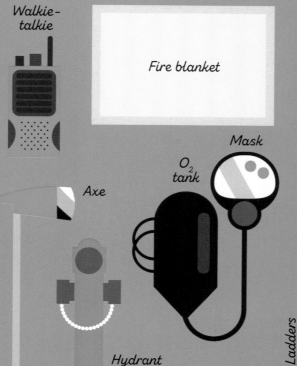

Axe

O_2 tank

Mask

Hydrant

Ladders

Fire blanket

Fire extinguisher

THE FIREFIGHTER'S TOP TIPS

Know your address

Know your exits

SMELL SMOKE OR SEE FIRE?

Tell someone

Get outside, never hide inside

If no one's around to help, call 999

Stay outside

Lifeguard

Have you ever seen lifeguards patrolling the beach or looking through binoculars? If so, you might think being a lifeguard looks pretty easy, but there's actually a lot of science in our job! Even if it looks fun, when we are on duty, we are always working and when someone needs our help we're ready to spring into action.

Our towers, chairs and huts are up high so we can see the whole beach. We look out to sea, scanning every spot and changing the patterns we look in, from right to left then from up to down, to stay alert.

Beach lifeguards have a lot of extra tools to help with our job. We use flags to warn swimmers about hazards such as **pollution** or rip currents, which can move around and be hard to notice.

When someone needs rescuing, we have special boards and floats to help bring them back to shore. Cool speedboats and motorised sea scooters can **propel** us to the rescue super-fast. Even with these awesome tools we lifeguards need to stay really fit, so we do a lot of swimming and exercise to keep us strong and confident in the sea. We are always ready to help!

> We're the experts in sun, sand, sea and surf safety!

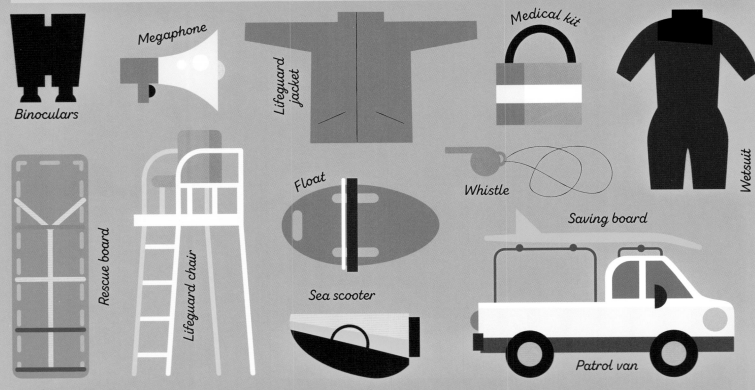

Binoculars

Megaphone

Lifeguard jacket

Medical kit

Wetsuit

Rescue board

Lifeguard chair

Float

Whistle

Saving board

Sea scooter

Patrol van

HOW TO SPOT A RIP CURRENT

Rip currents are like rivers in the ocean travelling out to sea from land. They are dangerous to get caught in because they might take you out to sea too! They're much easier to spot from above. There are clues to spotting rip currents and we need to recognise them.

Some breaking waves near the shore mean there could be a rip current nearby.

Different coloured water

Area of rough water on a smooth sea

Line of seaweed and debris moving out to sea

A gap in the breaking waves

There is always a rip near a pier or jetty

THE RIVER-LIKE RIP

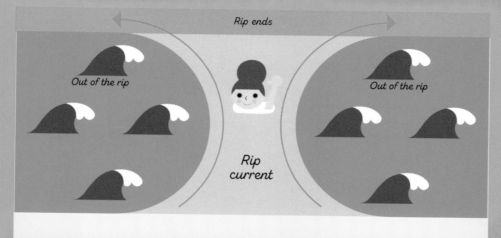

Rip ends

Out of the rip

Out of the rip

Rip current

Sometimes the water looks shallow and calm when a rip is there but you can quickly be carried off in its fast waters!

ESCAPE THE RIP

Even experienced surfers get caught in rips sometimes. If you find yourself in a rip, don't try to swim against it. Instead, focus on staying calm and go with the flow! This will save your energy. Signal with your arms and focus on breathing. When the rip stops pulling you out, you can swim along the shoreline and away from the area of the rip before swimming back in to land. Some rips even flow back to land, so don't panic!

CPR

A swimmer in trouble might be finding it hard to keep their head above water, so seawater might get into their mouth and airway. To help them we use CPR, which is a method to get oxygen to the lungs. It stands for Cardio (which means heart) Pulminary (which means the lungs) Resuscitation. We push down on the chest in a rhythm, and blow air into the person's lungs through their mouth or nose. It's pretty amazing stuff!

CPR isn't always needed so we do important checks first to make sure!

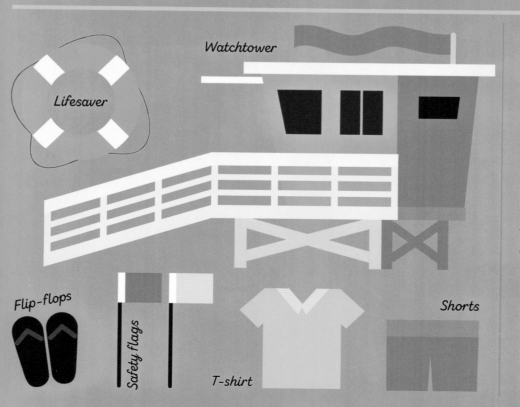

Watchtower

Lifesaver

Flip-flops

Safety flags

T-shirt

Shorts

Zookeeper

When you are a zookeeper you have to know a lot about the animals you care for. In the best zoos we create homes for the animals that are as close to their natural **habitats** as we can. These can be really varied! African hippos need ponds of shallow muddy water to bathe in all day long. They don't sweat like we do so wading in the water keeps their skin moist and cool. Spider monkeys need plenty of space and long branches to jump and climb on, just like the trees they would live in, in the wild.

There are foods that each animal can and can't eat. The green anaconda snake will eat a whole pig and then it doesn't have to eat anything else for a few months! Gorillas, on the other hand, snack a lot, but they stick to fruits and green vegetables. Animals need to eat what their bodies can **digest**, otherwise they will get ill – just like we would.

Sometimes visitors can get quite close to the animals. In some zoos you can walk in the lemur enclosure. These curious little animals are small and because they don't hunt, have big claws or teeth and aren't poisonous, they aren't dangerous. You can't get close to a lion, shark or grizzly bear! Research zoos before you visit, to make sure they are safe, care for and respect their animals.

We learn the best way to care for animals as a zookeeper. We love the animals we look after!

Belt carabina

Key

Bamboo

Juicy steak

Falconry glove

Broom

Overalls

Fish bits

Walkie-talkie

Tough boots

Zoo uniform

Bucket

Dung bucket

Shovel

Whistle

Wellies

Pocket multi-tool

Birds

You are here

Mammals

Reptiles

Fish

Arachnids

Crustaceans

Insects

Echinoderms

Explore the zoo's paths to find out how different animals are biologically connected.

Invertebrates

Animal World ZOO

SAVE OUR SPECIES

Many **species** are now endangered in the wild because of humans hunting them or destroying their environment. One day they could be extinct, which means they will be gone forever. Zoos around the world work together, trying to breed animals and raise money to support **conservation** in the wild.

Smoothie Maker

Woooosh! Let's turn this blender to top speed and whip you up a smoothie. Drinking a smoothie is a great way to get more fruits and vegetables in your diet. They are full of the amazing vitamins and minerals our bodies need so we can walk, play and just be our awesome healthy selves! The colours of food are a clue to which vitamins and minerals are inside – that's why it's good to eat a rainbow of colours.

At the smoothie hut we add yoghurt, seeds and vegetables as well as delicious, sweet fruit ... the bigger the mix of things we add, the healthier the smoothie. **Protein** shakes full of milk and seeds are good for people who do a lot of exercise as they help to build up muscles and make them strong.

The other important bit is the blitz! The blades in the blender mix and chop all the ingredients and turn them into the smoothie. Imagine how long it would take to make a smoothie if we tried chopping everything with a knife! The spinning blades at the bottom of the blender whizz around so fast that one smoothie takes seconds! Just make sure the lid is on when you press the button, or the customers will be wearing the smoothie, not drinking it!

With our awesome blended drinks we are a one-stop shop for your five-a-day!

Plum

Red apple

Peach

Green apple

Blueberry

Celery

Cherries

Watermelon

Grapes

Tomato

Kiwi

Pomegranate

Spinach

Avocado

Beetroot

Raspberry

Strawberry

THE SHACK RULES

Never mix a fruit-only smoothie

Fruits are super healthy but they are sweet too, because they contain a lot of sugar. You need to mix that up with other healthy things.

Use the whole food … not just the juice.

You'll get loads of extra good stuff like **fibre** in there, which cleans your insides and helps you poo!

Make it tasty!

Try your favourite flavours and experiment too. How about some coconut milk or fresh ginger?

Put that lid on …

Otherwise you'll get smoothie on the ceiling! It makes the blender safe too – those blades **rotate** at super high speed!

THE BLENDER VORTEX

When you turn on the blender, the blades at the bottom begin to spin. They **liquify** what they collide with, slicing it at super speed. But the spinning blades also create a **vortex** in the liquid, as the liquid spins and rushes up the sides. The vortex pulls air and solids from the top down through the centre, making sure everything gets mixed in.

So when you mix up a smoothie, you're making a mini tornado. Far out!

LID ON — Blades

PRESS ON — *Spinning vortex* — *Spinning Blades*

MAGIC MIX — *Vortex pulls air in* — *Liquid up sides*

Curly kale · Mango · Banana · Pineapple · Orange · Tangerine · Cucumber · Carrot · Apricot · Peas · Ginger · Cauliflower · Lemon · Almonds · MILK · Peanut butter · Chia seeds · Yoghurt

Delivery Driver

We delivery drivers start our day at the local sorting office where packages have been arriving all night, coming in huge lorries from warehouses and stores. Then drivers like me deliver them right to your address!

When we are out on delivery, we don't want to get lost. We look up the address on the sat nav to see the clearest route – problem solved!

The sat nav is a computer, with maps stored on its memory. The maps are updated all the time, along with other information such as traffic and where the road works are. As we drive along we see our position move on the sat nav screen ... a bit like moving through a computer game!

The sat nav in all bikes, cars, phones and trucks use GPS. This stands for Global Positioning System and it's the name for the network of **satellites** in space that circle Earth and tell you where you are.

It's far easier to use this cool living map instead of a paper one. Without GPS, making deliveries is much slower and more difficult. Got to go ... boxes to deliver and post to post!

Beep beep! We use GPS to find our way around the city and get deliveries to you on time!

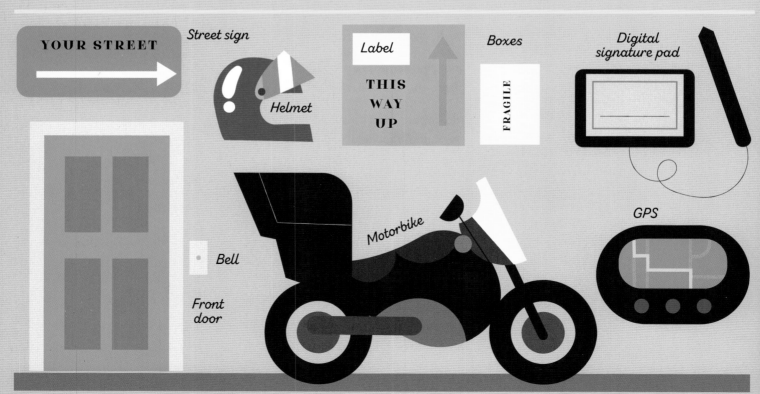

YOUR STREET

Street sign

Helmet

Label

THIS WAY UP

Boxes

FRAGILE

Digital signature pad

Bell

Front door

Motorbike

GPS

HOW THE GLOBAL POSITIONING SYSTEM, OR GPS, WORKS!

THE SATELLITE NETWORK

There about thirty GPS satellites in **orbit** around Earth and that's enough to provide everyone on the planet with their precise location. The same network of satellites is used by all sat nav devices, no matter the brand, age or where it is. There are lots of other satellites in different orbits around Earth doing different jobs.

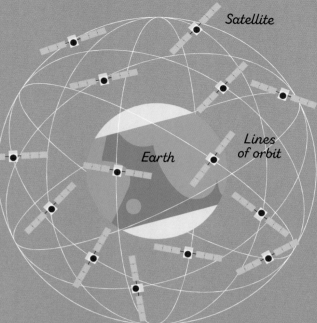

Satellite

Earth

Lines of orbit

Fun fact! It takes almost twelve hours for a GPS satellite to make one journey around Earth.

HELLO GPS

First, the sat nav uses signals from three of the GPS satellites and some clever maths to find out where you are. Now, just type in the delivery address ...

WHERE TO?

The computer searches its memory for routes and data. It then tells you the best route and you can begin your journey!

KNOCK KNOCK

With the GPS satellites updating your position all the time, your position on the sat nav updates too ... all the way to your destination!

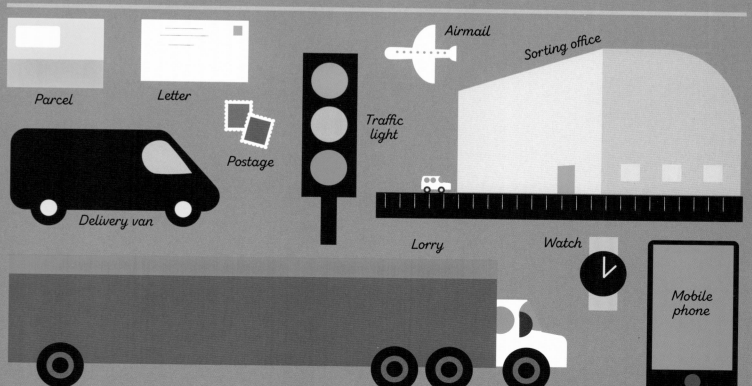

Parcel

Letter

Postage

Traffic light

Airmail

Sorting office

Delivery van

Lorry

Watch

Mobile phone

Hair Stylist

Snip snip! There are all kinds of ways to cut and style your hair. At the salon we aim to give you a fabulous haircut as your hair is always on show.

We have a lot of training before we are allowed to style hair. There are classic haircuts to learn, such as bobs, layers and creating fringes at the front. People have different kinds of hair too, like thick and curly or fine and straight. Whatever the type, we learn to cut it the right way so it stays in a nice shape and doesn't get damaged when we trim it.

When you come into the salon, we chat about what might suit you. People bring pictures of what they would like from magazines or the internet.

Then we wash or wet and brush the hair. Next, we cut using sharp scissors for precision. The scissors go in a special liquid between appointments, which keeps them free of **germs**.

Adults and teens often dye their hair, and we have dyes to turn hair into a rainbow of colours. It seems like magic but we do this using **chemical reactions**. It changes the hair's colour for good, but hair eventually grows out, so if the customer changes their mind they just have to wait. Take a seat and let's have some fun!

> We use colour chemistry to create marvellous hair make-overs!

Neck brush

Diffuser

Hairdryer

Comb

Mirror

Brush

Clippers

Thinning shears

Scissors

Razor

Chair

Gloves

Hair straighteners

Pintail comb

Section clips

Smartphone

Kirby grips

Bib

IN THE MIX

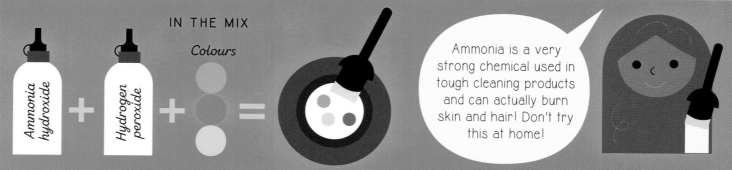

Colours

Ammonia hydroxide + Hydrogen peroxide + =

Ammonia is a very strong chemical used in tough cleaning products and can actually burn skin and hair! Don't try this at home!

First, we add our colours to the two base chemicals. The chemicals inside the liquid slowly start reacting. For the colour change to work, we need to brush the mixture on to the hair while the reaction is still taking place. So we mix it up just before painting all along the strands of hair. The dye changes only the parts of hair it touches. Then we leave the chemicals to work ...

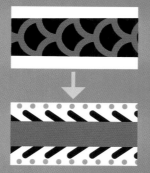

OPEN SESAME

The ammonia hydroxide makes the hairs puff up, and this creates little openings all the way along the hairs.

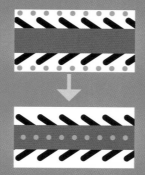

THE SNEAKY BIT

Tiny **molecules** of colour in the mix can now sneak inside the hair through the little openings!

KABOOM

Chemical reaction! The colour molecules puff up so much inside the hair they can't get out again!

COLOUR STAYS PUT

RINSE

We wash the chemicals out of the hair and the colour has been locked inside and the hair has changed for good!

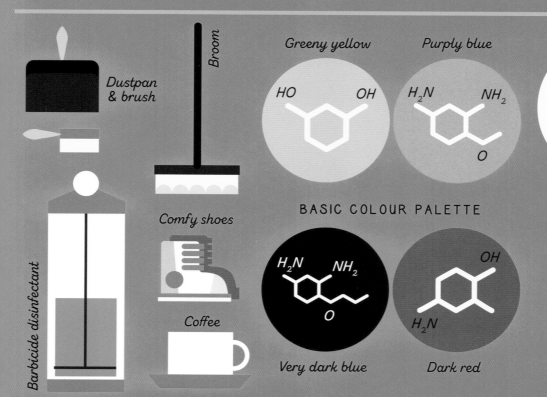

Dustpan & brush

Broom

Comfy shoes

Coffee

Barbicide disinfectant

Greeny yellow

Purply blue

We need to know how to mix the right colour so our customers don't end up with green hair when they asked for red!

BASIC COLOUR PALETTE

Very dark blue

Dark red

THE COLOUR CHEMISTS

Hairdressers mix up colours a bit like you might mix paints, but we can't see exactly how it will turn out at the mixing stage. We can't use just one colour either, as we always need a mix for our chemical reactions ... getting colour perfect is a real skill!

Ship's Captain

A captain could be in charge of a ginormous cruise ship, a sailing tall ship or a huge battleship! It is our job to make sure our **vessel** isn't damaged on its journey, and that all the passengers and cargo are safe on the seas.

Some voyages can take a long time – months, even – and we travel to some very distant parts of the world. It is dark at night as we are far from **artificial** light, and there are no unusual shapes or buildings to spot at sea, so we use GPS to help us find our way.

We rely on **marine radar** to map the vast landscape of mountains and epic canyons under the surface – it's similar to what's on land but often much bigger! Radar also detects obstacles such as reefs that could puncture the hull, or sandbanks that we could get stuck on. It also detects boats and large icebergs that are nearby. Small pieces of iceberg called 'bergy bits' are too small for radars, so the crew always keeps watch with binoculars.

At port, we drop the anchor and get everyone ashore. Then it's time to load up and chart a new course … bon voyage!

We understand the physics to know how to keep our ships afloat!

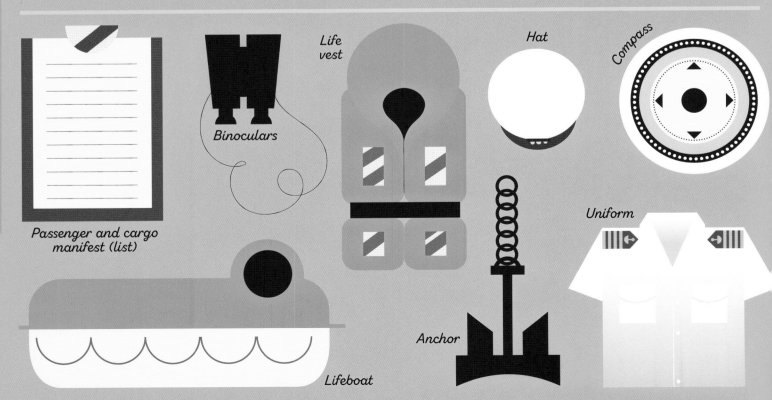

Passenger and cargo manifest (list)

Binoculars

Life vest

Hat

Compass

Anchor

Uniform

Lifeboat

HOW BOATS (AND ICEBERGS) BOB

Scientifically speaking, a ship is always sinking and floating at the same time! A ship sits with part of its hull in the water and part floating out of it. Even though ships are built from steel – a dense, heavy material – they will float as long as the total **density** of the ship is less than water. Ships' hulls are shaped to be filled with a lot of air, which makes the whole ship less dense than water, so it floats. This is why we always look after the hull. If a hole is made in it, the water gets inside and increases the density of the hull, and the ship will sink.

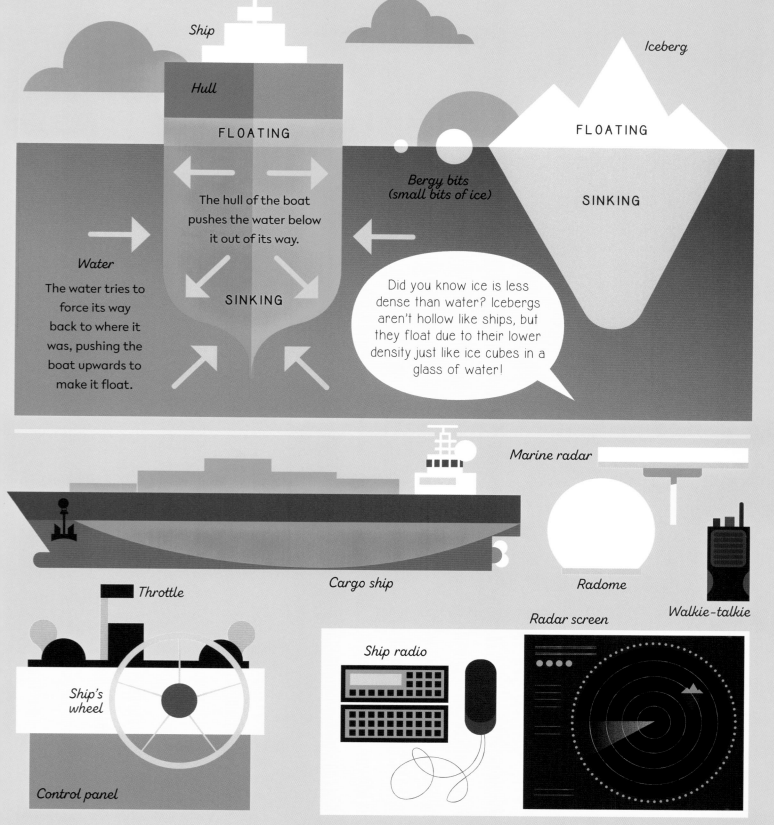

Ship

Hull

FLOATING

The hull of the boat pushes the water below it out of its way.

Water

The water tries to force its way back to where it was, pushing the boat upwards to make it float.

SINKING

Iceberg

FLOATING

Bergy bits
(small bits of ice)

SINKING

Did you know ice is less dense than water? Icebergs aren't hollow like ships, but they float due to their lower density just like ice cubes in a glass of water!

Marine radar

Cargo ship

Radome

Walkie-talkie

Radar screen

Throttle

Ship radio

Ship's wheel

Control panel

Baker

At our bakery we make all kinds of breads and cakes. Every **recipe** is different, but one thing all cakes and breads need is to be light. We do this by adding air bubbles! They get trapped in the mixture before baking to make a delicious light sponge or squishy roll.

We add air to cakes and breads in different ways, and they give different results. Imagine eating a slice of bread (mine's with peanut butter) and then a nice big slice of cake (raspberry jam and buttercream, please!). Apart from the flavours, the **textures** are very different. Cake is soft and melty all the way through, but bread is chewy and stretchy with a nice crust. Bread bubbles are also bigger and more varied in size than the teeny, regular bubbles of the cake sponge.

So how do we catch the air bubbles? In the cake mix it's the fats from butter and eggs that trap the air. Bread doesn't contain these **ingredients** though, so requires something extra – and that's kneading and time! Kneading is turning the dough, stretching and pulling it inside a big mixer or by hand. When you knead dough, **gluten** inside the flour begins linking together into very long chains. It's these super long, **microscopic**, stretchy gluten strands that trap air bubbles in bread. Yum, fresh bread!

It's the chemistry in our baking that creates our fluffy cakes and chewy breads!

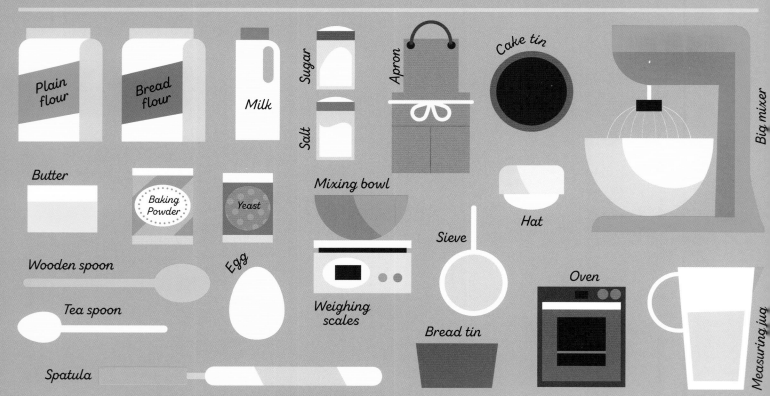

Plain flour

Bread flour

Milk

Sugar

Salt

Apron

Cake tin

Big mixer

Butter

Baking Powder

Yeast

Mixing bowl

Hat

Wooden spoon

Egg

Sieve

Tea spoon

Weighing scales

Oven

Spatula

Bread tin

Measuring jug

RECIPES FOR MAKING AIR BUBBLES

Cake BUBBLES

Baking powder is the chemical that creates the bubbles in the cake batter. The heat of the oven starts the chemical reaction, releasing a gas called carbon dioxide, or CO_2. The fat from the butter and eggs traps the CO_2, creating lots of tiny pockets of air – like blowing up millions of tiny balloons! The cake is ready when the liquid mixture has dried out enough to become solid ... don't take it out too early!

Plain flour — Egg, Sugar, Butter, Milk + Baking powder + Heat = CO_2 bubbles!

Bread BUBBLES

The air bubbles in bread are also made from CO_2 trapped inside, but those bubbles are made by a totally different ingredient, called yeast. It releases CO_2 gas during a chemical reaction called fermentation. That happens during proving – just after kneading, when you give the dough time to rest somewhere warm. After a while the dough doubles in size because it is now puffed up with bubbles of air!

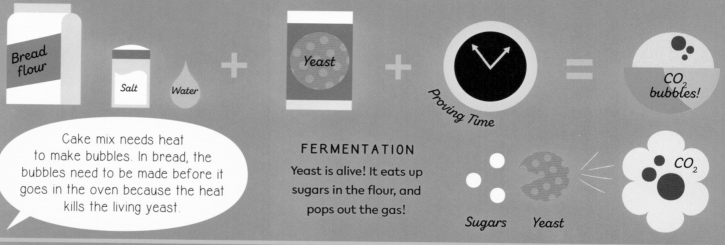

Bread flour — Salt, Water + Yeast + Proving Time = CO_2 bubbles!

Cake mix needs heat to make bubbles. In bread, the bubbles need to be made before it goes in the oven because the heat kills the living yeast.

FERMENTATION
Yeast is alive! It eats up sugars in the flour, and pops out the gas!

Sugars — Yeast — CO_2

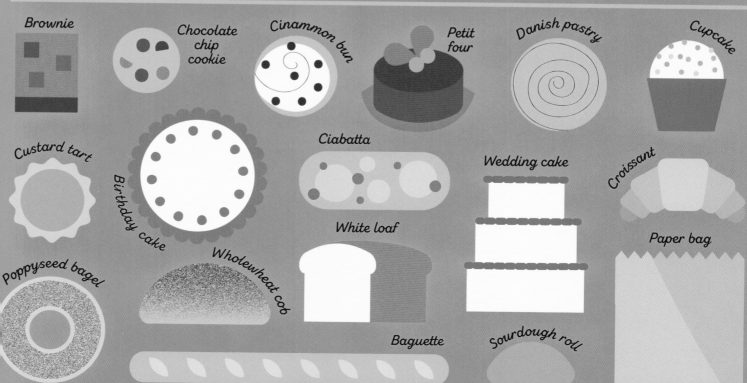

Brownie · Chocolate chip cookie · Cinammon bun · Petit four · Danish pastry · Cupcake · Custard tart · Birthday cake · Ciabatta · Wedding cake · Croissant · White loaf · Paper bag · Poppyseed bagel · Wholewheat cob · Baguette · Sourdough roll

Florist

Flower markets open very early in the morning, so we can buy flowers for the shop on the same day we will sell them. Cut flowers don't live long, so everyone works hard to get them from the grower to our shop, fast!

Some flowers are cut as buds, long before the flowers open, so that they blossom in the shop. We soak the cut stems in buckets of fresh water and add chemicals to kill any tiny **bacteria** that would eat away at the plant. If flowers are transported somewhere warm, they are sometimes kept cool in large fridges to stop them from **wilting**.

Many florists sell potted plants too, which need different care. Plants in a pot can live a long time because they aren't cut from their roots.

Whether they are cut or potted, all plants need water to drink, sunlight and space to breathe.

Some plants, like **succulent** desert plants, don't like much water. Bulb plants like daffodils and tulips like to be treated completely differently. They **bloom** in the wet and rainy spring so need lots of water to flower.

Botany is the science of plants and it helps me care for our plants and flowers.

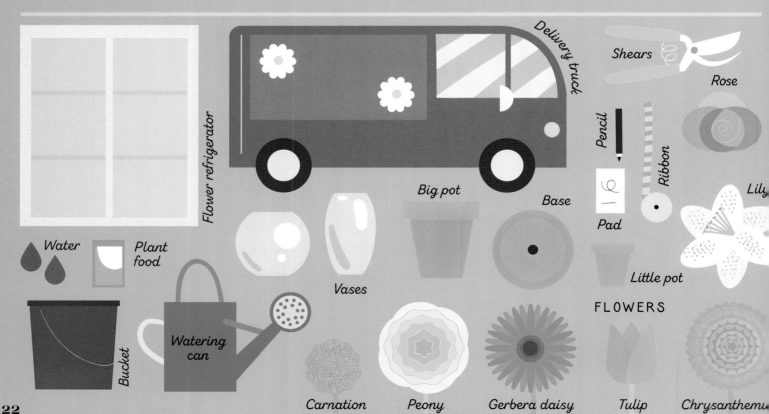

Flower refrigerator

Delivery truck

Shears

Rose

Pencil

Ribbon

Big pot

Base

Lily

Pad

Little pot

Water

Plant food

Vases

FLOWERS

Bucket

Watering can

Carnation

Peony

Gerbera daisy

Tulip

Chrysanthemum

FLOWER POWER: THE MAGIC OF LEAVES!

TIME TO EAT

Photosynthesis is the chemical reaction that plants use to make food. A plant needs sunlight, air and water for photosynthesis, and to stay healthy. The air and sunlight get in through the leaves. The water comes up from the roots through the stem.

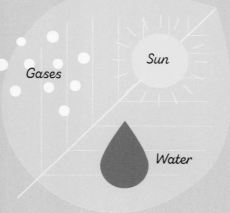

Gases

Sun

Water

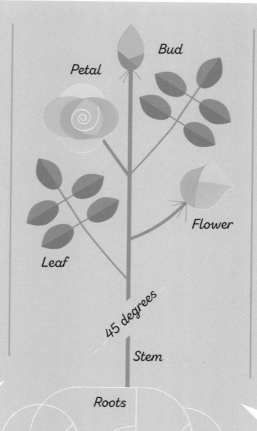

Petal

Bud

Leaf

Flower

45 degrees

Stem

Roots

As cut flowers are removed from their roots, florists cut the stems at a 45 degree angle. This helps the plant absorb water and nutrients faster than if they were cut straight.

WIDE, THIN LEAVES

A large, flat leaf has a bigger surface area for absorbing lots of sunlight for photosynthesis. There's also more room for lots of stoma, which are the tiny air holes that allow gases from the air in and out.

Since water travels up through the stem and out through the leaves, flowers need to keep drinking. Otherwise, the flowers dry out and die very quickly.

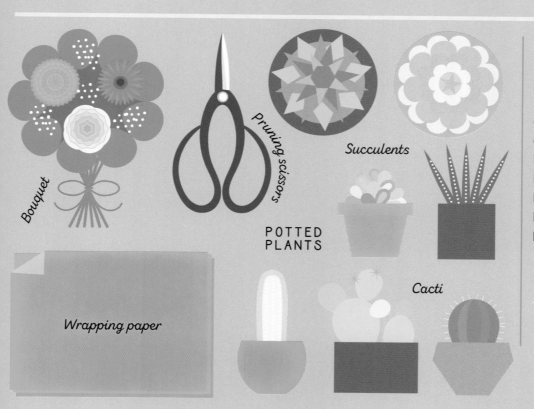

Bouquet

Pruning scissors

Succulents

POTTED PLANTS

Wrapping paper

Cacti

CHUNKY LEAVES

Some plants have special leaves to help them live in very dry places. They have thick leaves with less surface area to lose water from. Their leaves are often waxy to protect the water inside, a bit like wearing a raincoat but to keep water in. Hairs on the leaf help trap moisture **droplets** too. Some leaves even store food inside, which helps when the ground is very dry.

Plants like this can survive a long time at home in small pots, but be careful not to over-water them!

Doctor

How are you feeling today? We can help you feel well because we understand how the different **systems** of the human body work together.

When you visit your doctor, we use a secret science called the 'clinical method' to help our patients.

First is observation: we ask you questions and take a look at you. We have lots of tools in our bag to help us with this, such as our stethoscope.

Next is questioning: we think about what might be happening. We use our knowledge from training and consider things such as if it is flu season.

The next stage is called hypothesis: we come up with an idea of what might be making you feel poorly. We might do some tests, such as a blood test, to find out more. When we have all the information we need, we look at the results and put all the information together to make a **conclusion**, or a final diagnosis. When we have a diagnosis, we know how to treat you!

We know all about anatomy and how your body works, and use scientific thinking to make you better when you're ill.

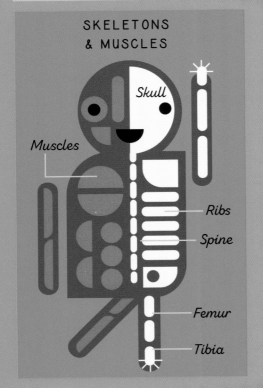

SKELETONS & MUSCLES

Skull
Muscles
Ribs
Spine
Femur
Tibia

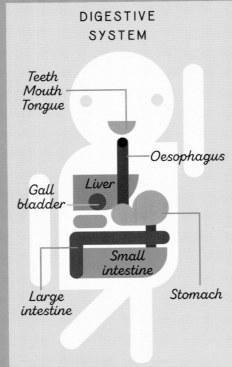

DIGESTIVE SYSTEM

Teeth
Mouth
Tongue
Oesophagus
Gall bladder
Liver
Large intestine
Small intestine
Stomach

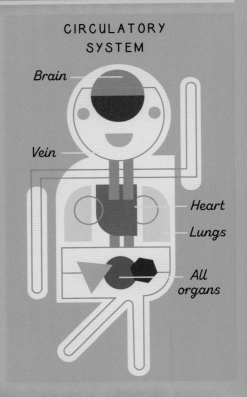

CIRCULATORY SYSTEM

Brain
Vein
Heart
Lungs
All organs

WHAT'S IN A DOCTOR'S BAG?

Small torch
This is used to test how the eye reacts to changes in light.

Peak flow meter
This measures how well you can push the air out of your lungs – like blowing candles out on a birthday cake!

Reflex hammer
Tests tendon reflexes. Your tendons join your muscles to your bones.

Thermometer
Measures temperature.

Stethoscope
For listening to your heart and lungs.

Sphygmomanometer
Measures blood pressure.

Otoscope
This is for looking inside the ear.

Tongue depressors
Holds your tongue down so we can look all the way into your throat.

4.0

Glucometer
This measures sugar in the blood. Too much sugar in our bodies isn't good for us.

These instruments are to help doctors make a diagnosis, so don't worry if a doctor carries out tests on you ... they are just collecting as much information as they can.

AT THE SURGERY

Prescription pad

Pen

Antiseptic

Injection

Bandage

Hand sanitiser

Watch

Gloves

Medicine

Mask

Computer

Cast

Crutches

Plaster

Cotton balls

Dog Groomer

Welcome to the doggy salon! If you love bubbles and working with dogs this is the place for you! Lots of different dogs visit the salon. The really hairy ones might need a haircut, or want a super slick **blow-dry**. Whatever they need for their makeover, first we have to wash our furry friends' fur.

Dogs don't need a proper bath as often as you do because they do a pretty good job of cleaning themselves, but it's still good to wash away any dirt and bacteria they might be carrying around. Mostly these aren't harmful, but there are a few nasties that can pass from the dog to you when you touch them – that's why it's good to wash your hands after stroking and cuddling them.

We bathe dogs in our special sinks, which are designed so the dogs can't slide around! This makes them feel comfortable and happy. We use the special shower to hose them with lovely warm water, and when they're nice and wet it's time to add the bubbles!

We squirt on some shampoo and give the dogs a good scrub. The soap lifts away all the dirt into the bubbly **lather**. After that we shower off the soap down the plug hole, leaving pup ready for some pampering!

The science of shampooing helps us get dogs clean and happy!

Towel

Apron

Razor

Dog scissors

Fluffy Pomeranian

Lead

Shower hose

Dog bath

Shaggy tall dog

Dematting comb

Puffy sheepdog

HOW SHAMPOO (AND OTHER SOAP) WORKS

ADD WATER

Hosing down a dog with water will definitely wash out some of the dirt and **grime**. But the oil and dirt won't all get washed away. Instead, it clings to the dog's skin and fur, because they are oily too! Oil and water **repel** each other – they don't mix well at all!

Fun fact! It's the heads and tails of the soap molecules that create bubbles too!

Water

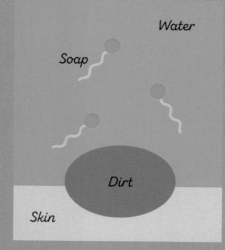

Water

Soap

Dirt

Skin

SHAMPOO

Soap molecules have two ends. The head end is drawn towards water and the tail end is drawn towards oily dirt and grime.

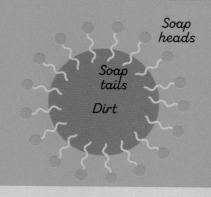

Soap heads

Soap tails

Dirt

BUBBLE UP

As the tails are drawn to the oily dirt, the soap surrounds it, creating lots of little dirt droplets. These carry the dirt away from the skin, into the water.

AND RINSE

Then all we need to do is wash the soapy water away! A good blow-dry and brush, and you've got one happy, clean pup!

Ribbon

Short-haired pup

Brush

Long-haired terrier

Nail clippers

Dryer

Gloves

Mucky Pup

Flea -B- Gone

Best In Show

SHAMPOO FOR DOGGOS

It's important to wash dogs with things that are kind to their skin, otherwise it will be dry and itchy, which is very uncomfortable! All skin is made of layers of **cells**, and these wonderful tiny cells protect our bodies from germs and bacteria. The very top layers keep moisture in, which is a big part of keeping skin healthy. A dog's top layer of skin is less thick than ours, so their skin is a bit more delicate, and dries out more easily. We have our own range of shampoos for dogs, made just for them!

Traffic Officer

Beep beep! A traffic officer's day at work can be very noisy. Cars and trucks rumble along city streets and whizz by on busy motorways. It's our job to make sure everyone drives safely.

Imagine if cars were going along one road at lots of different speeds – they'd be bumping into each other! So, each road has a speed limit to show the fastest a car can drive there. A road beside a school will have a slow speed limit (perhaps as low as 5 mph), because lots of people are about or small children may run out. On a motorway there are no bikes or pedestrians, so it is safe for cars to travel much faster – at up to 70 mph!

Sometimes people don't like driving slowly because it makes journeys take longer. But accidents with faster cars are more deadly, and it takes longer to slow down or stop in an emergency, so it's important people follow the speed limits. Speed cameras by the roadside photograph vehicles going too fast and send a letter to the car's owner with a **fine**. We can also catch speeding cars with our hand-held speed guns!

When we direct traffic in busy city streets we use hand signals. They are useful as drivers might have their radio on or windows up, and traffic is noisy, so sign language is a great way to communicate. Keep an eye out and stay safe on the road!

Our tools use physics to catch people who speed!

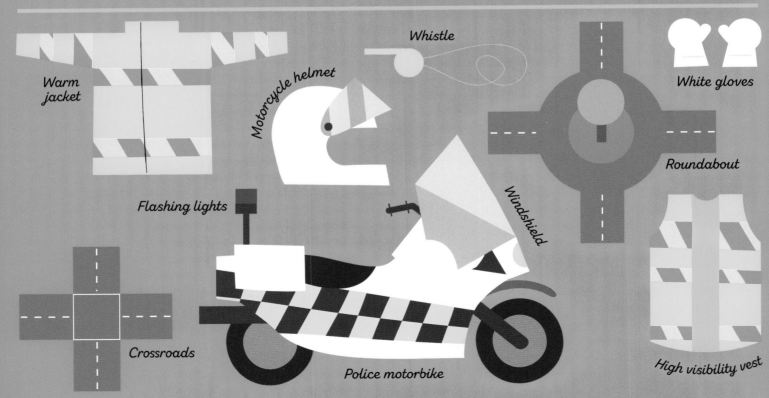

Warm jacket

Whistle

White gloves

Motorcycle helmet

Roundabout

Flashing lights

Windshield

Crossroads

Police motorbike

High visibility vest

READING THE WAVES

Speed guns use a clever physics discovery to detect car speeds. It is called the Doppler effect, and you can hear it with your own ears! Have you ever noticed the changing sounds a car or train makes as it passes you? The sound is more **high-pitched** as it comes towards you and then it sounds **lower pitched** as it moves away. The sound hasn't really changed at all – it's just the Doppler effect! It's all about the sound waves and this is how it works.

We must be standing still for the gun to read the speed accurately. The Doppler effect is affected by our position too!

STOPPED STEADY

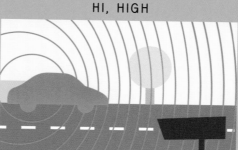

Sound travels in vibrations or waves. When the car's motor is running and you are standing still, the sound of the engine does not change. It's a bit like humming one note ... have a go!

HI, HIGH

When the car is coming towards you, the sound waves become more squished together – this makes the noise we hear sound more high-pitched. Now try humming a bit higher.

GOING LOW

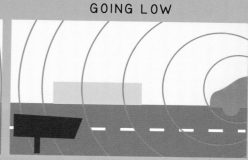

When the car is travelling away from you, the waves stretch and also lose energy the father away the car is. The sound gets lower and lower until it's gone. Have a go at this to mimic the Doppler effect!

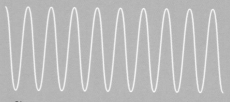

Sound waves

Close-together waves = high-pitched sound

Far-apart waves = low-pitched sound

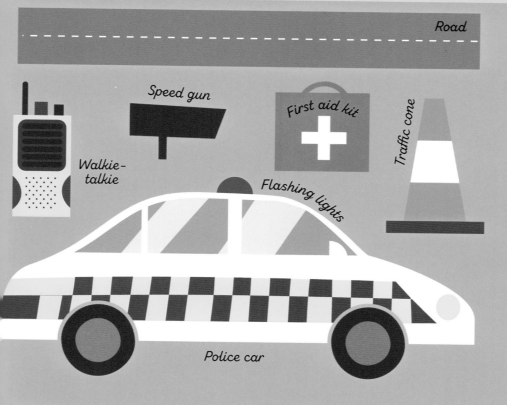

Road

Speed gun

First aid kit

Traffic cone

Walkie-talkie

Flashing lights

Police car

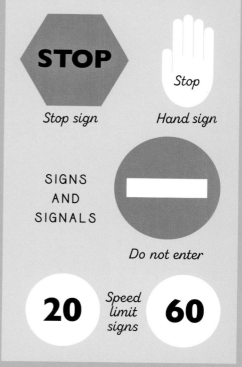

STOP

Stop sign

Stop

Hand sign

SIGNS AND SIGNALS

Do not enter

20 Speed limit signs **60**

Glossary

Here are some words from the book that you might not know!

Artificial – made by humans and not found in nature

Bacteria – very small living things made of just one cell

Bloom – when a flower opens

Blow-dry – drying and styling hair with a hairdryer

Cell – very small building blocks of all living things

Chemical reaction – when a substance changes and becomes a new substance

Conclusion – the most likely explanation based on the information available

Conductor – an object that allows heat or electricity to travel through it

Conservation – protecting an area from damage by humans

Density – how tightly packed together something is

Digest – breaking down food in the body to take out the nutrients

Droplet – a small drop of liquid

Fibre – parts of food that the body cannot digest

Fine – a payment made for breaking a rule

Fire-resistant – protects from fire

Germs – a very small living thing that causes disease

Gluten – two proteins together that make food stretchy

Grime – dirt that is stuck on a surface

Habitat – the natural home for a plant or animal

High-pitched – a high sound

Ingredient – an item of food that is needed to make a dish

Lather – frothy bubbles made by soap and water

Liquify – turning a solid object into a liquid

Lower pitched – a low sound

Marine radar – marine means to do with the ocean and radar is a way of finding objects using radio waves

Microscopic – so small that you need a microscope to see it

Molecule – a very small unit that is part of a solid, liquid or gas object

Orbit – a curved path that an object follows when it circles around another object

Poisonous – will make you very unwell or even kill you

Pollution – human waste that damages nature

Propel – pushing forward

Protein – a nutrient that provides fuel for the body and helps it grow

Recipe – instructions to make something such as a cake

Repel – pushing away

Rotate – turning around

Satellite – a piece of technology that flies in the sky, receiving and sending back information

Smothering – to cover completely

Species – a group of animals that share common features

Succulent – very juicy and full of liquid, also a type of plant

System – the way that things work together

Texture – the way something feels when you touch it

Vessel – a boat, also a container that carries something else

Vortex – when air or liquid flows around in a tight, spinning circle

Wilting – when flowers or plants lose too much water and can no longer stand up straight

#ScienceSquad

Now you have discovered that science is everywhere, here are some ways you can become part of the science squad too.

Dedicate a whole day to science. On that day, try and look for these key scientific concepts all around you.

Living things that grow

Chemical reactions

How objects feel to the touch

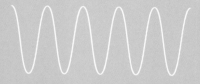

Sounds and how they travel

Patterns and changes in the weather

Things changing between solid or liquid or gas

Technology that helps you do something difficult

Names for similar objects and groups of objects

Make a #ScienceSquad notebook out of scrap paper and write down or draw what you find. Rank your discoveries in order from most surprising to least surprising. Where was the most unexpected place or time that you came across science in your day?

Question Time

Interview an adult or grown-up friend of the family about the everyday tasks they do in their job or at home. Take some notes in your #ScienceSquad notebook and compare against the everyday science above. Can you find some unexpected science in their day? You might surprise even them!